I0803672

THE MOSSAD

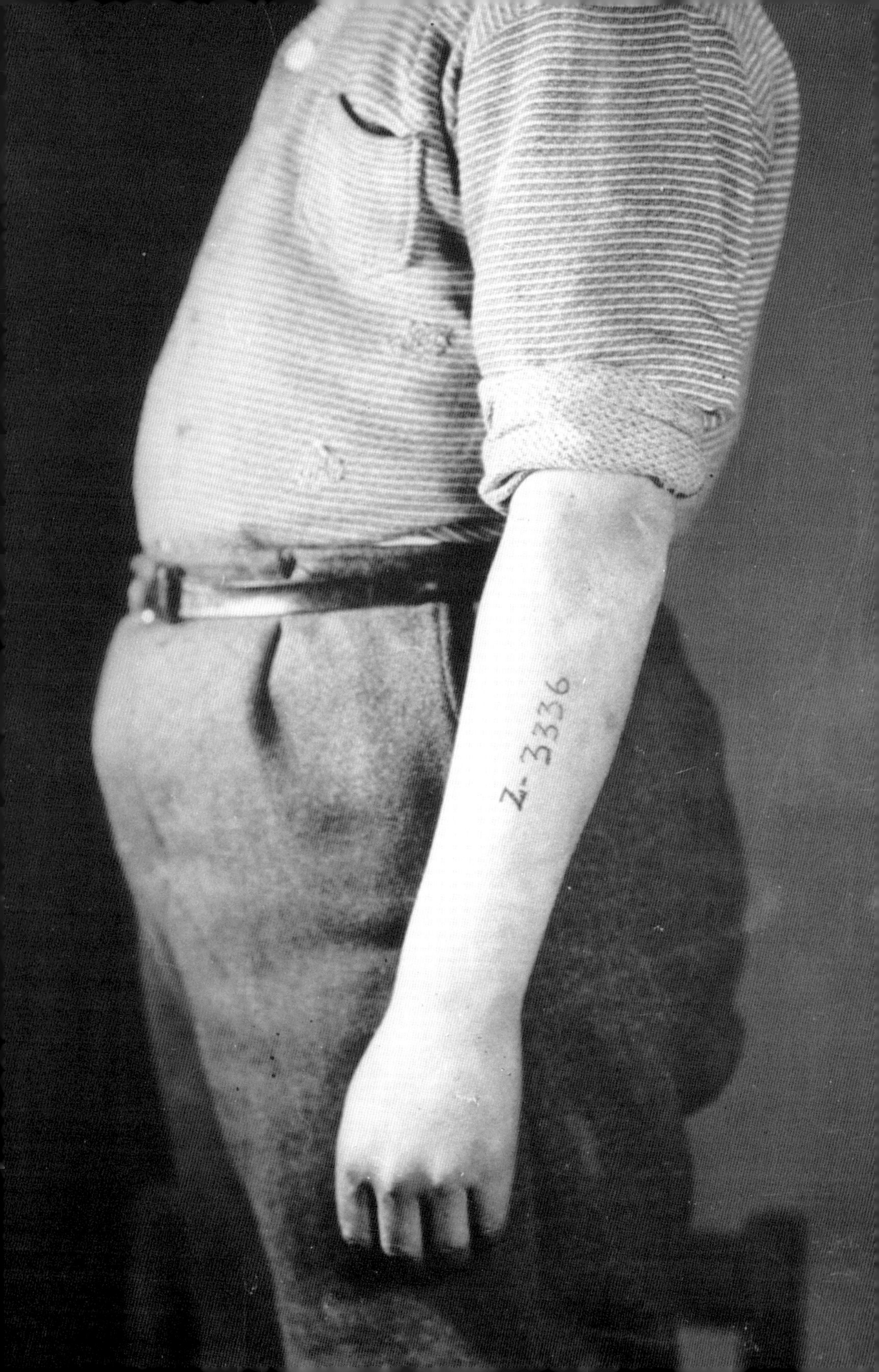
Z-3336

THE MOSSAD

ODYSSEYS

KRISSY EBERTH

CREATIVE EDUCATION · CREATIVE PAPERBACKS

Published by Creative Education and Creative Paperbacks
P.O. Box 227, Mankato, Minnesota 56002
Creative Education and Creative Paperbacks
are imprints of The Creative Company
www.thecreativecompany.us

Design by Graham Morgan
Art direction by Tom Morgan
Edited by Jill Kalz

Images by Images by Getty Images/AFP, 75, Co Rentmeester/Time Life Pictures, 64, Denver Post, 19, DigitalGlobe, 58, duncan1890, 14–15, GALI TIBBON, 31, Keystone, 54, Keystone-France, 11, MPI, 6, RAMZI HAIDAR, 53, ullstein bild Dtl., 2, Universal History Archive, 8–9; Unsplash/José Martín Ramírez Carrasco, 27, Julius Wiebe, 24–25; Wikimedia Commons/Anonymous, 41, Dean Calma/IAEA, 34–35, Government Press Office (Israel), 60–61, IDF Spokesperson's Unit, 69, Israel Press and Photo Agency (I.P.P.A.)/Dan Hadani collection, National Library of Israel, 44–45, Israeli Defense Forces Spokesperson's Unit, 28, public domain, cover, 70–71, SDASM, 20, Tim Bessler, 4–5, unknown author, 48, 50, ןואיזומ רואמ רינ ל"את סיה ליחו הלפעהה, 12

Library of Congress Cataloging-in-Publication Data
Names: Eberth, Krissy, author.
Title: The Mossad / Krissy Eberth.
Description: Mankato, Minnesota : Creative Education and Creative Paperbacks, [2025] | Series: Odysseys in spycraft | Includes bibliographical references and index. | Audience: Ages 12–15 | Audience: Grades 7–9 | Summary: "Unlock the spy secrets of the State of Israel's Institute for Intelligence and Special Operations (Mossad), from the espionage agency's history to counterterrorism training and key missions. Includes a glossary, sidebars, index, and further resources"— Provided by publisher.
Identifiers: LCCN 2024018506 (print) | LCCN 2024018507 (ebook) | ISBN 9798889892915 (library binding) | ISBN 9781682776575 (paperback) | ISBN 9798889894025 (ebook)
Subjects: LCSH: Israel. Mosad le-modiʻin ṿe-tafḳidim meyuḥadim—Juvenile literature. | Intelligence service—Israel—Juvenile literature. | Espionage—Israel—Juvenile literature. | Spies—Israel—Juvenile literature.
Classification: LCC JQ1830.A56 I633 2025 (print) | LCC JQ1830.A56 (ebook) | DDC 327.125694—dc23/eng/20240426
LC record available at https://lccn.loc.gov/2024018506
LC ebook record available at https://lccn.loc.gov/2024018507

Printed in the United States of America

Wiretapping, or bugging, telephones was easier in pre-mobile days.

CONTENTS

Introduction

On May 14, 1948, only hours after the State of Israel was established as a country, five neighboring Arab nations attacked, hoping to wipe it out. The attackers had far more soldiers and weapons than Israel but underestimated how much information Israeli spies had already gathered about the Arab nations' military capabilities and strategies. The war quickly turned in Israel's favor.

OPPOSITE: Military strength combined with an arguably unmatched way of obtaining enemy secrets makes Israel a strong fighter.

Israel's survival from 1948 to today has depended on it maintaining a well-established **intelligence** network to gather secret data, carry out **covert** operations, and fight terrorism. At the heart of this network is the Mossad, a shadowy organization charged with keeping Israel safe from outside enemies by any means necessary.

The Mossad is known for the efficient, calculating, and notoriously aggressive way it carries out missions. In 1973, for example, a group of Mossad special forces went to Beirut to commence the mission named Operation

Intelligence concerning the military has been the domain of a security branch called Aman since Israel's early days.

OPPOSITE Palestinian politician Kamal Adwan was killed in his apartment during the 1973 Operation Spring of Youth raid.

Spring of Youth. The mission's goal was to eliminate leaders of a terrorist organization. The leader of one of the Mossad hit teams dressed up as a female tourist. He snuck into the area with a gun and grenades hidden beneath his dress. When all team members were in place, he gave the signal. The teams charged, eliminated their targets, and stole important intelligence documents. Once the combat part of the mission was finished, Israeli Air Force helicopters picked up the Mossad special forces and sped them back to Israel.

Agency Origins

Espionage has a long and glorious history in Israel. According to the Bible, before the Israelites crossed into the land of Canaan in their journey from Egypt, their leader Joshua sent out spies to scout the area around Jericho. The intelligence that the spies gathered helped the Israelites conquer the town and begin building their first kingdom.

OPPOSITE: Reaching back to Biblical times, armies understood that knowing their enemies' secrets was half the battle.

More than 3,000 years later—even before Israel became an official nation in 1948—Jewish settlers in the British-controlled region of the Middle East then called Palestine formed underground groups to push for more Jews to be allowed to enter the region. Their activities intensified as millions of European Jews were slaughtered by German Nazis during World War II (1939–45). Jewish groups around the world began pushing for the creation of a safe haven for Jews. Arab countries in the region opposed this idea and threatened to destroy any Jewish state that was established. The Arab-Israeli War that began in May 1948 was designed to carry out that threat.

By the early 1950s, Israel's first prime minister, David Ben-Gurion, had created a three-prong intelligence network to protect the new country from the enemies that surrounded it. One prong of the intelligence network, named Aman, would handle military intelligence, gathering data about enemy forces and weaponry that might threaten Israel. A second institution, Shin Bet, would be responsible for security and counterintelligence within the country, much like the Federal Bureau of Investigation (FBI) in the United States.

The third prong, the Mossad, whose Hebrew name translates as "the Institute for Intelligence and Special Operations," would have the widest-ranging responsibilities. These would include gathering intelligence outside Israel's borders; preventing Israel's enemies from developing weapons; preventing or responding to terrorist acts against Israelis around the world; cooperating with espionage organizations in other countries friendly to Israel; and developing covert spy networks in both friendly and hostile countries.

The Mossad's reputation for being an efficient and sometimes deadly organization has been built on the "special operations" it has conducted. It has done everything it could to protect its country and citizens, including kidnapping an infamous Nazi war criminal in Argentina and sneaking him into Israel to be put on trial; avenging the 1972 murders of 11 Israeli Olympic athletes and coaches; coordinating a daring late-night rescue in Uganda of more than 100 Jewish passengers of a hijacked plane; and planting spies inside two enemy

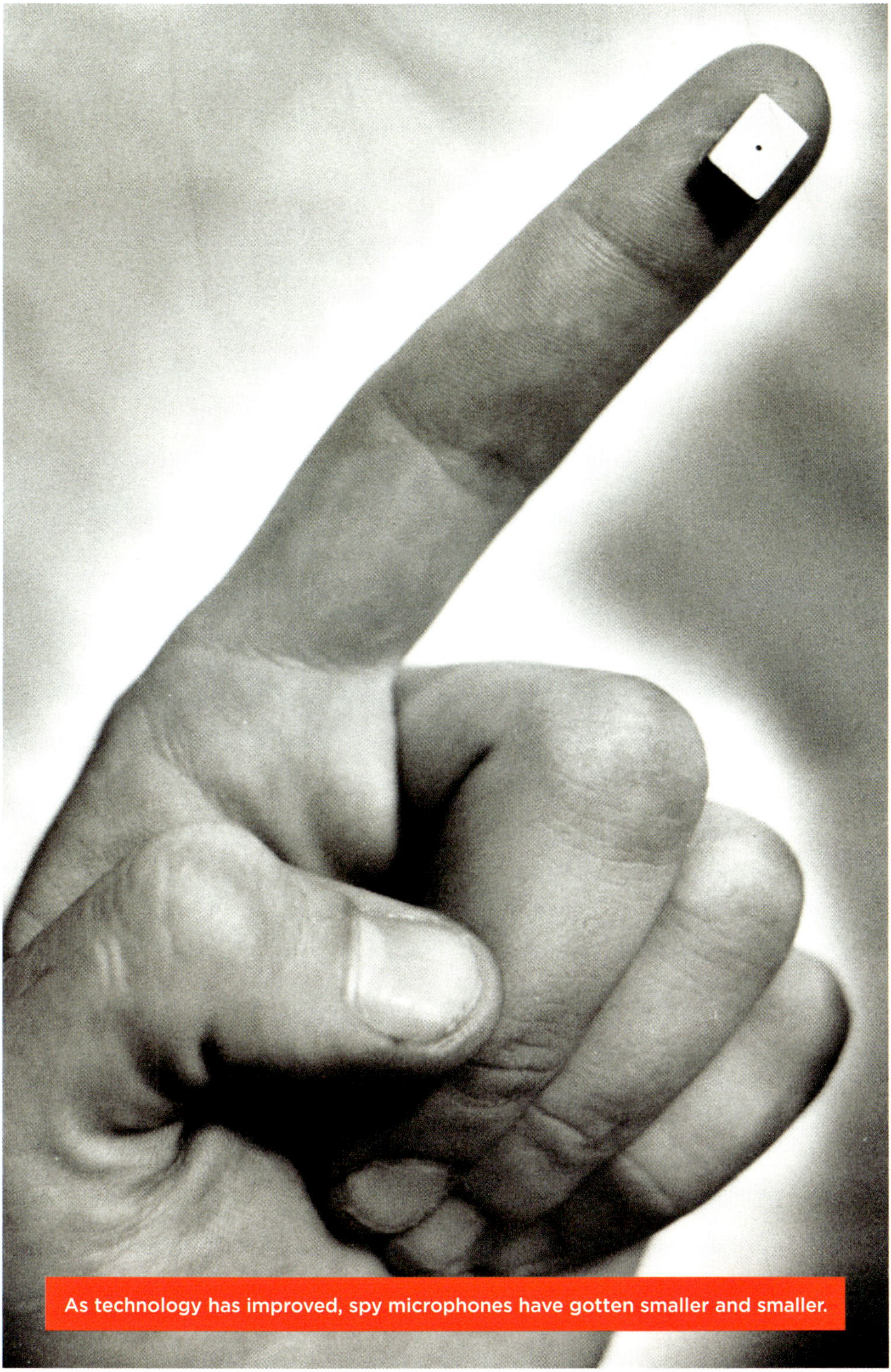

As technology has improved, spy microphones have gotten smaller and smaller.

Fly Away

In August 1966, the Mossad made headlines by stealing a Russian warplane being used in Iraq. Actually, the Mossad didn't steal the plane; an agent based in Baghdad convinced an Iraqi pilot to fly the MiG-21 to Israel. The agent scouted for several months and found a Christian pilot named Munir Redfa, who was openly unhappy with how Iraqi leaders treated non-Muslim people in the country. While Iraqi and Russian leaders were embarrassed by the defection, Israel and its allies eagerly inspected the latest model of Russian aircraft.

countries to provide the intelligence Israel needed to win a major war in only six days.

Like most intelligence organizations, the Mossad is secretive about its operations. The less enemies know about how the organization is run, the better off Israel will be. Some of the Mossad's secrets have gradually come to light, though. For example, it's now known that all employees are civilians, though most served in the military when they were younger. Most work within Israel, near the organization's headquarters in Tel Aviv. Mossad **operatives** based in other countries often live undercover, using false identities.

The Mossad carries out its duties through eight separate departments. The largest is the Collections Department, which gathers intelligence data sent by spies from around the world. Other departments coordinate planning and operations, communications, research (especially concerning nuclear capabilities of other nations), technology, and political cooperation with governments friendly to Israel. The most secretive department is known by the Hebrew name Metzada, meaning "fortress." Its work, as described in the British journal *Jane's Intelligence Review*, involves "small units of combatants who carry out actions abroad against those considered to be a threat to Israeli security. . . . These missions have included assassinations and **sabotage**." The assassination squads have their own name, Kidon, which is Hebrew for "bayonet."

The Mossad has had a lot of success in placing **agents** throughout the Arab world. These spies have helped thwart hundreds of attacks. The Mossad is the second largest intelligence agency in the Western world. Its staff

"THE ASSASSINATION SQUADS HAVE THEIR OWN NAME, KIDON, WHICH IS HEBREW FOR 'BAYONET.'"

of more than 7,000 employees and budget of around $3 billion give it immense power. The head of the Mossad reports directly to the Prime Minister of Israel. In the past, the commander of the Mossad was kept a secret, as were most of the agency's details. But in 1996, Israel announced the appointment of Major General Danny Yatom to head the Mossad. And to keep up with the times, the agency has created a website and a Facebook page. These communication tools help with **recruiting**.

Living in the Shadows

Based solely on Hollywood movies, a spy's life is always action-packed and often glamorous. Fictional undercover killing machines such as Jason Bourne and handsome, smooth-talking agents such as James Bond have almost superhuman powers. Many TV shows and movies have Mossad characters and are based on real Mossad operations. Examples include Ziva David in the hit television series *NCIS* and the 2018 movie *Operation Finale*, based on a Mossad operation to capture a Nazi war criminal. But what is life really like for a Mossad agent?

OPPOSITE: No matter where a spy is, they must be able to blend in and avoid drawing attention.

Working as a spy is dangerous and stressful. If spies are discovered, the governments or groups they are spying on may jail or even execute them. Seemingly innocent mistakes can prove costly. To help avoid detection, Mossad agents posing as citizens of a foreign country are cautioned to wear clothing and shoes from that country only. Strange but true, being caught with Israeli-made underwear in an Arab country has tripped up several Israeli spies and led to their capture.

Most real-life spies are not as attractive or as daring as the actors portraying them onscreen. Espionage agencies purposely look for average-looking people who can blend in with those around them. Agents are usually of ordinary height and build. Most are also able to speak several languages. A Mossad agent should be fluent in Arabic and English as well as Hebrew, and knowledge of Russian can also be helpful.

Successful spies are unidentifiable and untrackable.

Big Screen

The Mossad is such an interesting spy agency that movies are made about its missions. A 2019 movie called *The Red Sea Diving*

Considering the risks involved with the job, what makes people want to be spies—or agree to become spies against their will? According to American journalist and espionage expert Ernest Volkman, the reasons can be summed up with the acronym MICE. The letters represent the words *money*, *ideology*, *compromise*, and *ego*. Some people become spies because they are paid well for the information they uncover and transmit. Others become spies because they have a strong belief in their country or in the ideals represented by another country. Others may be blackmailed, or compromised, into spying to avoid punishment or to prevent some dark secret about themselves from being revealed. Still others may think that becoming a spy is the way to show off how clever or daring they can be.

There are several types of spies, and not all live or act the same. Spies working in another country fall into two categories: legals and illegals. Legals work openly in their own country's embassy in a foreign country. As an official government employee, they are allowed to bend some rules of the nation in which they are working. If legals are caught spying or trying to recruit others to spy for them, they are usually sent back to their home country rather than jailed.

Illegals are spies who assume false identities and work undercover. If they are caught, their punishment often takes severe forms, from torture to execution. Some illegals create elaborate cover stories about themselves to conceal their spying activities. **Moles** are a kind of illegal. As the name implies, moles live an underground existence. They work secretly inside an enemy's intelligence service or top-secret facilities. They often work for their own country's intelligence agency but reveal confidential information to another country. The Mossad has a long history of recruiting moles who have access to data that Israel wants and of setting up secret identities and fake companies for moles placed in enemy nations.

A **double agent** works for two different spy agencies. In most cases, a double agent is someone who has been caught spying for an enemy and coerced into sending

Passports used by Mossad agents

back wrong intelligence, called disinformation. A double agent may also be a spy who decides to switch sides for money or because of a change in beliefs.

An **asset** is a hidden source acting as a spy or providing secret information to a spy. Assets are very important to agencies such as the Mossad. They do the real undercover spying, while the Mossad agents often act as handlers, transmitting secret documents and photographs back to Israel and making sure the assets get paid for their work.

Some spies volunteer for the job. They may discover things going on that they believe should be revealed or stopped by supplying secret information. Men and women in the military may also volunteer to spy for their country, or they may become **traitors** and reveal secrets to an enemy. In general, agencies such as the Mossad do not accept volunteers. They recruit the agents they need within Israel or in other countries. That's how naval officer Victor Ostrovsky joined the Mossad.

In April 1979, Ostrovsky, a Canadian-born Israeli, received secret orders to attend a meeting at a military base near Tel Aviv. When he arrived, Ostrovsky was led into a small office where a stranger in civilian clothes told him, "We've pulled your name out of a computer; you fit our criteria. You are already serving your country, but there's a way you can serve it better. Are you interested?"

Ostrovsky said yes and began an intense period of recruitment and training. As part of his recruitment process, Ostrovsky was questioned at length. The questions included: "Would you regard killing somebody for your country as something negative?" and "Is there anything

Disappearing Act

A Mossad trick helped Israel build its first nuclear weapons in the late 1960s. To produce fuel for the weapons, Israel needed a large supply of uranium ore, but no country would sell it to Israel. A Mossad operative established a business relationship with a chemical company in Belgium and persuaded one of its owners to order 200 tons (181 metric tons) of uranium ore and then ship it to another company in Italy. Between Belgium and Italy, the ship made an unscheduled stop. When it finally docked (in Turkey), its cargo consisted only of empty barrels.

D-301
BRUTTO 253,1KG
RADIOACTIVE II
UN 2912
D-301
RADIOACTIVE II
UN 2912
D-301
RADIOACTIVE II
UN 2912
D-301
RADIOACTIVE II
UN 2912
D-30
BRUTTO

more important than freedom?" Ostrovsky later learned that several thousand men and women had been interviewed to make up a training class of only 15 people.

Throughout the next two years, Ostrovsky and the other recruits were warned not to reveal anything about themselves to one another. They were even instructed to make up new names and to put together a believable new personal history. "Keep yourself to yourself," they were told. Recruits learned a variety of spy skills, or **tradecraft**. They learned how to code and decode messages; how to

“WOULD YOU REGARD KILLING SOMEBODY FOR YOUR COUNTRY AS SOMETHING NEGATIVE?”

tail others and recognize when they were being followed; and how to use spy cameras, radio detection finding (RDF) equipment, and other secret instruments. Most of all, they learned how to blend in to get the information they wanted while avoiding detection. In other words, they learned how to live successfully in the shadows.

Tools of the Trade

The purpose of espionage is to gather and send information that someone else wants kept secret. For most of human history, intelligence collection was done directly by individuals using deception and trickery and few other tools. In spy language, this is called HUMINT (human intelligence). Through the years, the Mossad has used deception as a key strategy in its missions. They have been known to use disguises and false identities to achieve their objectives.

In the 20th century, spies began using more tools and technology to help them obtain information. In the 1950s, the Mossad developed a tool that could cut keys. It was operated by the motor of a sewing machine. This tool was used to create duplicate keys to allow agents to break into houses, offices, and other areas without being caught. Technology such as cameras, hidden microphones, and computers soon transformed the spy world. Today, the Mossad and other spy agencies gather ELINT (electronic intelligence) via the Internet and computer monitoring or hacking; SIGINT (signal intelligence) by intercepting radio, telephone, and other communications; and PHOTINT (photographic intelligence) by studying photographs taken by spy planes, satellites, or human operatives. These methods fall under the heading of TECHINT (technical intelligence). Modern spies need a wide range of technical skills and support. Learning to use electronic gadgets has become an important part of their tradecraft.

Because Israel is one of the world's leading countries in developing computers and electronic devices, the Mossad has a ready supply of high-tech tools at its disposal. One tool is a powerful computer program called Promis. This program is used to break into electronic systems around the world to uncover terrorist plots and ensure national security. Israel has never admitted to the existence of Promis, but its use has been reported by journalists who cover intelligence topics. These journalists have also reported that Israel has sold Promis systems to other countries in hopes of hacking into various security databases. Such reports have never been officially confirmed, however.

Another piece of advanced technology used for Israeli security is the Iron Dome. Israel developed

Herbert Cukurs

Never Forget

The Mossad agent Yaakov "Mio" Meidad was a German-born Jew whose parents were killed in Nazi death camps during World War II. In the 1960s, the Mossad learned that a Nazi named Herbert Cukurs was living in South America. Cukurs was responsible for the deaths of 30,000 Latvians during World War II, and Meidad was tasked with hunting him down. Known as "the man with the hundred identities," Meidad was able to befriend Curkurs and eventually convinced him to become a business partner. With trust established, the Mossad struck. On March 7, 1965, Cukurs's body was found inside a crate in Montevideo, Uruguay. A note attached to his body read, "We Can Never Forget."

it to defend the country from missiles launched at it from short range. The Iron Dome was created in large response to the conflict between Israel and Hezbollah. Hezbollah is a militant group based in Lebanon. In 2006, Hezbollah launched thousands of rockets at Israel causing tremendous damage and loss of life. Israel vowed to create a system that could defend its people. The Iron Dome system uses radar to track incoming missiles and identify if the missiles will hit a populated area. Rockets are then fired by the Iron Dome to intercept and destroy them. Israel first used the Iron Dome in 2011, when it intercepted a missile fired from the Gaza Strip. Since then, it has been in constant use. According to the Israel Defense Force, the Iron Dome had a success rate of 97 percent during a 2022 confrontation with Islamic terrorists firing from the Gaza Strip.

While TECHINT tools play a key role in the Mossad's work, simpler HUMINT tools also have their place. Modern spying often involves combining the two to accomplish a goal. Miniature spy cameras enable Israeli operatives and moles to photograph secret actions or documents. Some of these cameras can be concealed in a spy's coat button, watch, or pen and operated via a wireless connection. Mossad agents also use small, sophisticated **bugs**. These usually contain a microphone, transmitter, and antenna. Once the bug is hidden in a room or wired into a phone line, a spy can tune to a specific radio frequency to eavesdrop on a conversation or record a telephone call. It is even possible to bug someone's cell phone by sending a message with a computer virus.

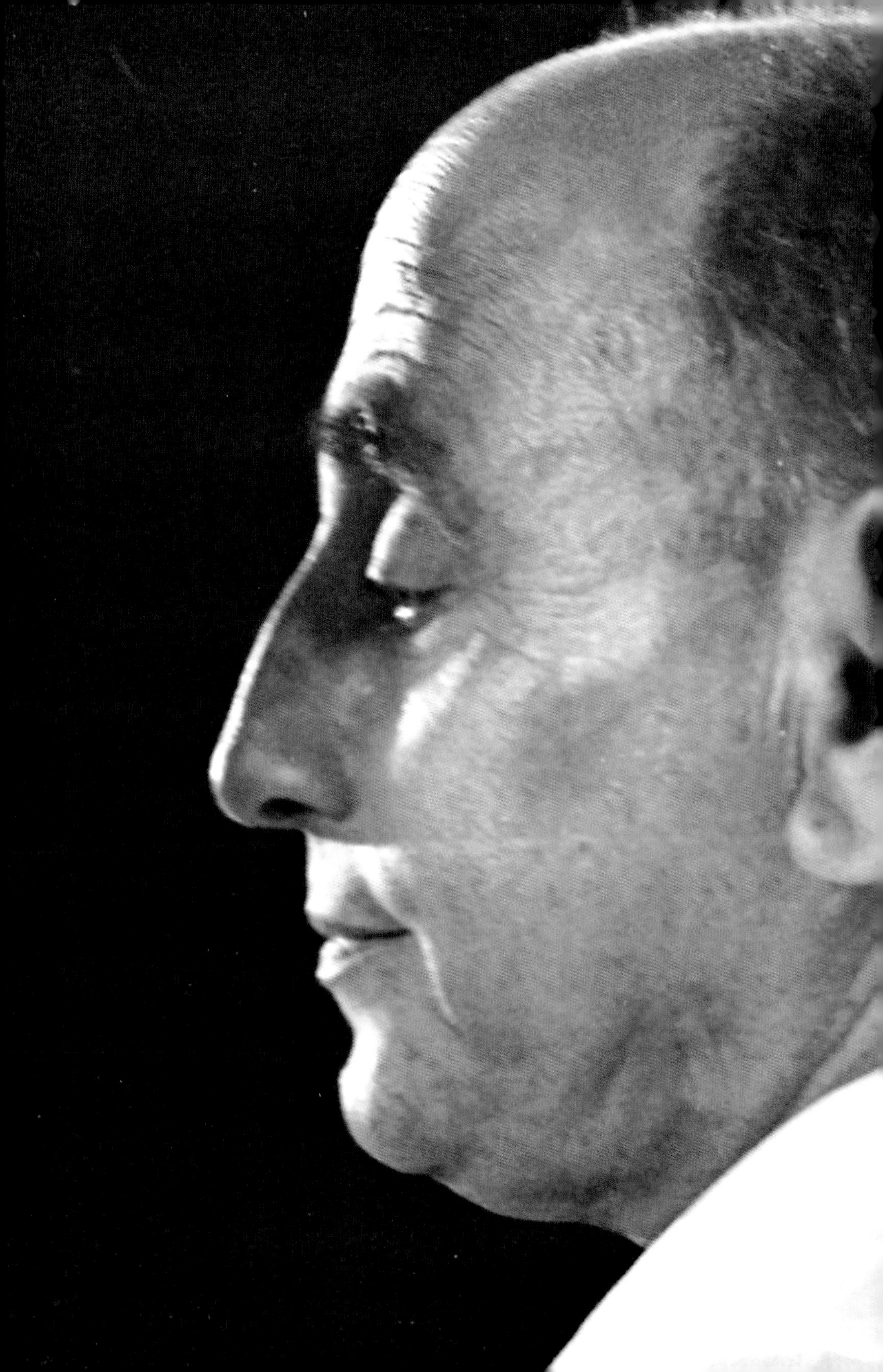

Notable Agents

Spies need to know how to see without being seen and how to uncover secrets while revealing little about themselves. No one was more secretive than Isser Harel, Israel's first spymaster. Harel immigrated to Palestine from Latvia in 1930 when he was 18 years old. He showed his talent for espionage even then by smuggling a gun past British military agents. They never suspected that the 4-foot-8 (142-cm), innocent-looking young man might be hiding a weapon.

OPPOSITE: Isser Harel (1912–2003)

Over the years, many of Israel's enemies would underestimate the talents and determination of "Isser the Little." In the late 1930s, Harel joined the intelligence wing of the Haganah, the Jewish underground army in Palestine, spying on the British forces occupying Palestine. In 1948, Harel was asked to organize and lead Shin Bet, the internal security service, and then to become director of the Mossad in 1952, where he served until 1963. During those years, none of Harel's friends and neighbors knew exactly what he did for a living. His secretive nature became legendary. His colleagues told a joke about a taxi ride he once took. When the driver asked Harel where he wanted to go, Harel replied, "I can't tell you. It's a secret."

While Harel was a spymaster in Israel, two of his most important operatives were living dangerous undercover lives in enemy countries. Eli Cohen and Wolfgang Lotz were two of the most famous and successful spies for the Mossad. The information provided by both men would be vital to Israel's lightning-quick victory over Egypt and Syria in the 1967 Six-Day War—though one would be executed and the other imprisoned by the time fighting broke out.

Eli Cohen was an Egyptian-born Jew who could easily pass for an Arab. In 1955, Cohen traveled to Israel and volunteered to become a spy. He worked first for Aman and then for the Mossad. Needing an operative in Syria, the Mossad sent Cohen for training in Argentina, where he built an elaborate cover for himself as a Syrian businessman named Kamal Amin Ta'abet. Many wealthy Syrians were living in Argentina in the late 1950s, and Cohen/Ta'abet befriended them. He built trust and

Eli Cohen

received letters of introduction to powerful people in Damascus, Syria, where he moved in 1962.

In Damascus, the Mossad helped Cohen set up a fake textile import/export business, and he began sending goods throughout Europe. The seemingly successful businessman was soon invited to gatherings of Syrian political and military leaders and even went on tours of several Syrian military bases. He set up a radio transmitter in his apartment and sent out coded messages relating details of the Syrian military setup. He also took photos, which he transferred to microfilm, and made copies of top-secret documents on Syrian troop movements and locations of warplanes. He hid the evidence in hollowed-out legs of pieces of furniture he shipped to Mossad **drops**.

Over time, Cohen became careless, though. He often made his radio transmissions at the same time

Following Eli Cohen's hanging, anti-Israel writings were draped on his body.

every evening. The radio activity was discovered by Syrian security using RDF equipment, and Cohen was captured. He was given two choices: become a double agent or be tried and hanged. He took the second choice and was executed in 1965 before a cheering crowd in Damascus. Still, the Syrian military secrets he uncovered would prove invaluable two years later.

Wolfgang Lotz was a German-born Jew who came to Palestine to escape the Nazis. He fought with the British against the Germans in Egypt during World War II, where he mastered Arabic and English. The Mossad approached him about becoming a spy in Egypt. "I was blond and stocky and the very epitome of an ex-German officer," he explained. Lotz was sent to Germany for training and to help establish his cover story as an ex-Nazi who wanted to set up a horse ranch in Egypt. Then, in 1960, he moved to Cairo.

Like Cohen, Lotz befriended important political and military leaders. Once, he was taken on a tour of an Egyptian missile facility where his guide said, "The Israelis have an excellent intelligence service. They must not learn about our rockets until we strike a blow with them. Now, let me show you around."

Lotz telegraphed reports to Tel Aviv and made several trips to Paris, France, to meet with his Mossad contacts. Then he, too, became sloppy, and his radio transmissions were detected by Egyptian security in February 1965. He was arrested but protested that he was not Jewish and was spying only for the money. He was sent to prison and later returned to Israel as part of a prisoner exchange.

The information supplied by Cohen and Lotz helped the Israeli military learn just where to strike the most

Operation Sphinx

In the late 1970s, Israel became convinced that Iraq was building a nuclear weapons factory near Baghdad. The Mossad began a secret campaign to make sure the factory never became operational. Nicknamed Operation Sphinx, the campaign included the recruitment of an Iraqi nuclear scientist working in France as a mole, bombings at French and Italian factories supplying Iraq with parts, and even an unsolved murder of an Egyptian nuclear scientist helping the Iraqis. Then, late one night in June 1981, Israeli fighter planes flew a 684-mile (1,100-kilometer) mission to Iraq and destroyed the plant, setting back Iraq's nuclear capabilities by many years.

Ashraf Marwan at his wedding to the daughter of the Egyptian president

Agent Angel

Ashraf Marwan was described by some as the greatest spy of the 20th century. Marwan was a well-connected Egyptian national. He was also the son-in-law to the Egyptian president. His family connections and business deals gave him access to sensitive information. In 1973, he warned the Mossad and Israel of an attack on Yom Kippur (a Jewish religious holiday) by the Egyptians and Syrians. This warning and Marwan's life was depicted in the 2018 movie *The Angel*. "Angel" was the code name the Mossad had given him. Marwan died suspiciously, falling from a balcony, in 2007.

devastating blows against Syria and Egypt. When war broke out among the three countries in June 1967, Israel struck quickly inside its enemies' territory, declaring victory a mere six days later.

Many times, the names of agents are unknown, but their actions are notable. In late 2006, Mossad spies tailed a Syrian government leader visiting London, England. They snuck into his hotel room and installed a device on his laptop computer that allowed them to steal data. The spies found detailed plans and photographs showing construction of a possible nuclear reactor disguised to look like an ordinary factory. Warning bells went off in Israel.

The Mossad placed a mole inside the Al Kibar factory. This spy began electronically sending photographs and videos that showed what was really going on inside. The Israelis shared their findings with U.S. intelligence and military leaders, who helped them determine exact coordinates for a possible bombing mission to destroy the site. (Throughout this time, Syrian officials denied the existence of any nuclear facilities in their country.)

Then a high-ranking Iranian military leader **defected** and agreed to tell members of the U.S. Central Intelligence Agency (CIA) what he knew about Iran's nuclear plans. He revealed that Iran was helping to fund a secret nuclear facility in Syria. The CIA passed the defector's information along to the Mossad.

Still, Israel felt it needed more proof before taking action to destroy the Syrian plant. Using low-flying helicopters to avoid radar detection, a team of technicians was flown into Syria to take soil samples to check for radiation in the Al Kibar area. They narrowly avoided capture by a Syrian patrol. Meanwhile, other spies reported that a North Korean ship was sailing toward Syria with suspicious-looking pipes on board that could be used to build a reactor. Intelligence also warned of another ship that would arrive soon with cargo full of uranium materials. This was all the evidence Israeli leaders felt they needed; they decided to act.

Late on the night of September 5, 2007, 10 Israeli aircraft took to the air, flying west over the Mediterranean Sea. This mission involved jamming Syrian electronics and destroying the nuclear research facility. The success

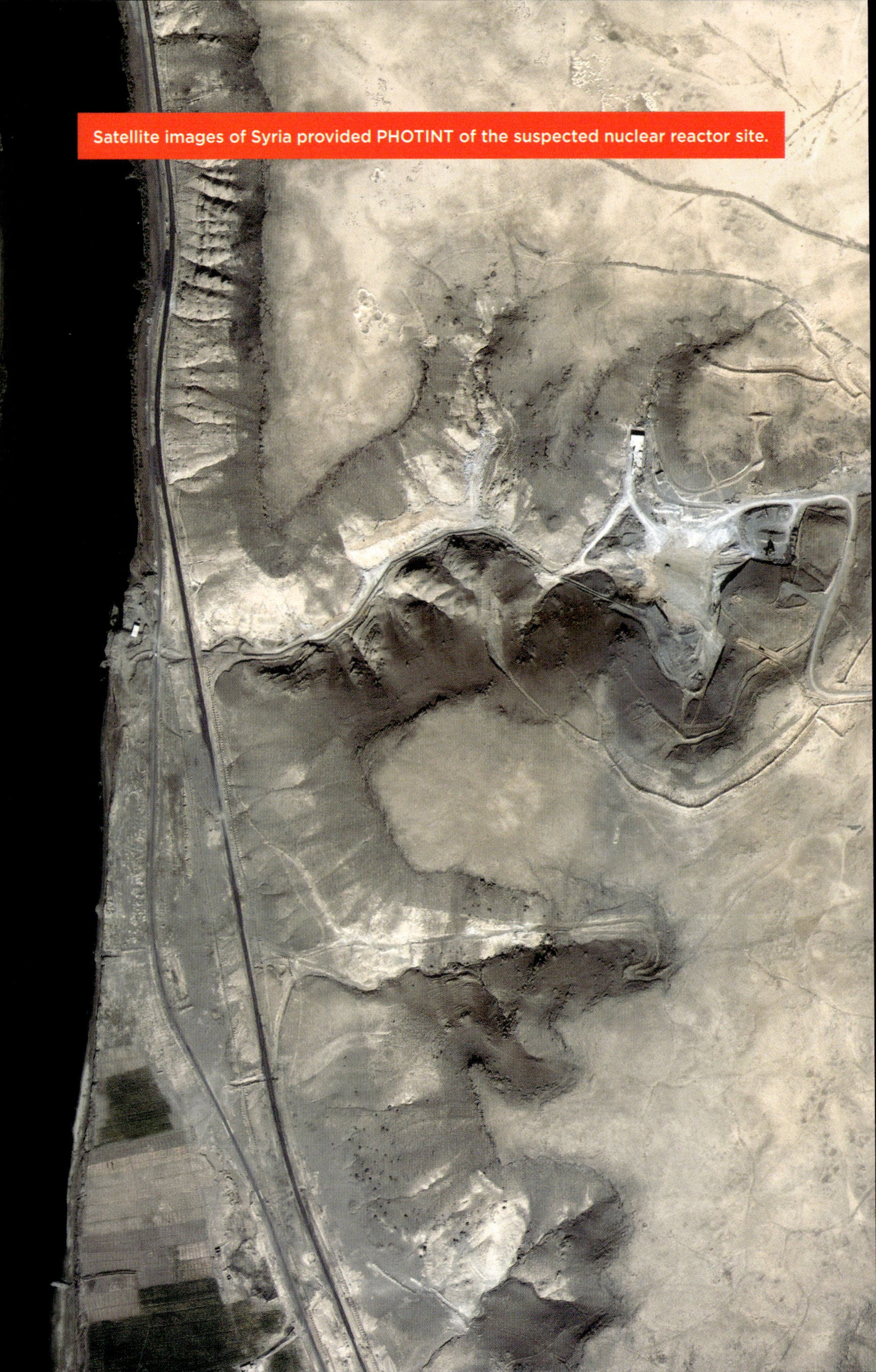

Satellite images of Syria provided PHOTINT of the suspected nuclear reactor site.

of the mission relied on the Israeli Electronic Warfare platform. This new technology shut down the Syrian defense systems and allowed the Israeli jets to fly undetected. At first, the jets appeared to be on a routine patrolling mission, and then seven planes peeled off and flew over Syria. With the bombing coordinates already programmed into their computers, the pilots flew over Al Kibar, wiped out the nuclear reactor, then flew home at top speed. Operation Orchard was a success.

Surprisingly, the bombing mission did not arouse much anger. Instead, the Syrians quickly cleaned up the debris and paved over the area so that no one, least of all United Nations weapons inspectors, could tell what had existed there before. It would be nearly two years before the story of Israel's spy work and bombing came to light.

On a Mission

Some of the missions that Mossad agents have carried out seem more like movie scripts than real life. In fact, several of them have been made into movies. For example, *The House on Garibaldi Street* (1979) is based on Isser Harel's account of how Mossad agents captured Adolf Eichmann, a former Nazi who was hiding in Argentina.

OPPOSITE: Nazi Adolf Eichmann paces in his cell after capture.

It took more than two years to locate Eichmann. He suspected he was being hunted and moved with his family several times to avoid capture. Finally, on May 11, 1960, he was grabbed in broad daylight while getting off a bus near his home on Garibaldi Street in Buenos Aires. He was taken to a secret location, where agents checked for Nazi tattoos and other characteristics that verified his identity.

Eichmann was kept closely guarded for 10 days. Meanwhile, a Mossad agent was planted in a local hospital, supposedly suffering from a brain injury. After a week of treatment by a doctor employed by the Mossad, the "patient" was released and given permission to fly home the next day on an Israeli plane. Eichmann's photograph quickly replaced the agent's photo on a fake passport, and he was disguised with bandages and rushed past airport security and onboard the plane. Within days, the world learned of Eichmann's capture, and Argentine leaders expressed great anger. But the mission had been accomplished. Eichmann was later tried and executed for his Nazi crimes.

The 2005 movie *Munich*, directed by Steven Spielberg, focuses on one of the most controversial missions Mossad agents ever carried out. The movie opens with the shocking massacre of 11 Israeli athletes and coaches by terrorists at the 1972 Summer Olympic Games in Munich, Germany. How Israel responds to the massacre is at the heart of the movie. Following the direct orders of Israeli prime minister Golda Meir, a Mossad "hit squad" hunts down and assassinates 12 members of Black September, the terrorist group that had carried out the murders. Israel seeks revenge, not justice. Slightly more than a month after the Olympics, the first

A masked terrorist stands guard during the Olympic massacre in Munich in 1972.

terrorist is gunned down in the lobby of his apartment building in Rome, Italy. Then, over the next 6 years, 11 other Olympic Games terrorists are killed through a variety of methods. Several are shot by guns equipped with silencers fired from cars or motorcycles. Others are killed in their apartments by remote-controlled bombs detonated by a telephone call and a radio transmission.

As bloodthirsty as these killings were, the Mossad might have escaped major public outcry, except for a huge mistake made in Lillehammer, Norway, in July 1973. Following a tip, a Mossad team arrived in Lillehammer, where it tracked down and then executed the suspected leader of the Munich terrorists. The victim strongly resembled the man they had seen in photographs. Unfortunately, he was not the terrorist. He was just a Moroccan waiter in the wrong place at the wrong time.

The mistake quickly came to light, and five members of the Mossad team were arrested by Norwegian police before they could flee the country. All were given relatively light sentences for the murder, but the damage done to the Mossad's reputation was significant. Nations around the world condemned Israel's actions, and other intelligence agencies scoffed at the Mossad's poor spy work.

An amazing Israeli spy and rescue mission several years later received much more positive response from people around the world. It is the focus of the 1977 movie *Raid on Entebbe*. The events took place in late June and early July of 1976 in the east-central African nation of Uganda. At the time, Uganda was run by a **dictator** named Idi Amin, who gave support to many terrorist groups.

On June 27, 1976, a group of terrorists took over an Air France plane flying from Israel to Paris with 250 passengers and crew aboard. They forced the pilot to fly to the Entebbe airport in Uganda. There, all non-Jews were released and flown back to Israel, but 105 Jewish hostages were kept under close guard inside the airport terminal. The terrorists said they would kill the hostages unless 53 terrorists were freed from jails in Israel and elsewhere by July 4, 1976. Israeli prime minister Yitzhak Rabin pretended that Israel would cooperate with the terrorists as a trick to buy time to undertake a rescue mission.

Meanwhile, Mossad spies based in Africa studied airport blueprints, handled all preparations needed for the rescue party, and made sure no one in Uganda suspected that a raid was in the works. Other agents interviewed the freed hostages to learn more about the airport setup. Meanwhile, Israeli military and intelligence leaders organized the operation. This was the plan: Approximately 200 soldiers would fly nearly eight hours in cargo planes, land in Uganda without being detected, get inside the terminal where the hostages were being held, wipe out the terrorists before they could shoot any hostages, rush the hostages onto the escape plane, and take off for Israel. Mission leaders gave themselves only one hour to carry out the raid itself. Any more time would give Amin's army time to attack the rescuers. A full-scale rehearsal was held in Israel to get the timing right, and then the mission was a go.

Amazingly, the raid at Entebbe took exactly 58 minutes and resulted in only 4 Israeli casualties—3 hostages died in the gunfire that ensued, and the leader of the mission was killed by a Ugandan sentry as he led the hostages to the plane. The daring rescue was a perfect

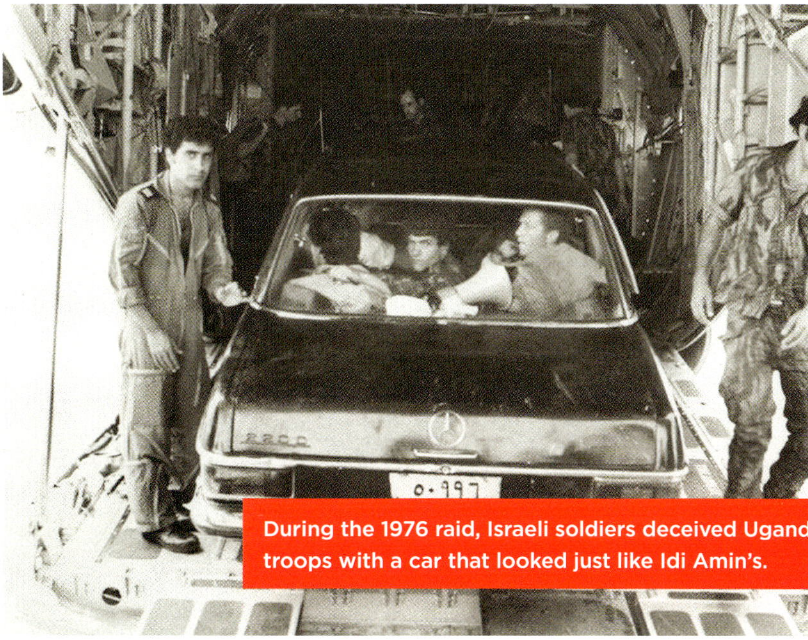

During the 1976 raid, Israeli soldiers deceived Ugandan troops with a car that looked just like Idi Amin's.

example of how spies and military leaders could work together to combat terrorism successfully.

The Eichmann capture, the Olympics revenge plot, and the Entebbe rescue mission all illustrate the independence and determination of Israel's intelligence community. They also show that the tiny Middle Eastern country is willing to take a lot of risks to do things its own way. Some mistakes have been made, and Israel has often been accused by other countries of being reckless—even by its closest ally, the United States. Israel's

Arab Setbacks

In one year, 2007, several Middle Eastern Arab countries suffered serious, mysterious setbacks in their efforts to possess nuclear and chemical weapons. A nuclear plant under construction in Syria was bombed. An explosion at a chemical weapons factory in Syria killed dozens of skilled technicians. Trucks delivering weapons from Iran to the extremist militant group Hezbollah in Lebanon was blown up before it crossed the Iranian border. Puzzling malfunctions occurred in nuclear facilities in Iran. No one claimed responsibility for any of these events, but all were probably the work of Mossad operatives.

leaders do not seem concerned by the criticism. They believe that to protect a country surrounded by large, powerful nations intent on its destruction, they can't always play by the rules.

In 2008, Iran was suspected of developing nuclear weapons. This time, the Mossad decided to stop Iran by attacking computers at the nuclear plant, a tactic called cybersabotage. The mission was titled Operation Olympic Games. Mossad agents developed a computer virus that would **infiltrate** Iran's computers. The software would infect only the computers that were using the software Mossad intelligence identified as controlling the nuclear system. The Iranians were wary of such a virus and, to be safe, kept their nuclear reactor offline. The Mossad had to send an agent into the facility on a mission to physically insert a thumb drive into one of the computers. The virus then sabotaged the mechanical reactors of the nuclear plant, making them overheat and destroying much of the facility. In July 2020 and April 2021, the Mossad launched second and third attacks at this same Iranian nuclear site, attacks that blew up most of the site.

On October 6, 2023, the Palestinian group Hamas carried out a huge surprise attack on southern Israel from Gaza. Some reports say more than 5,000 rockets were launched, while Hamas fighters used boats and paragliders to breach the Israeli border. Terrorists invaded an open-air concert and went house to house, attacking Israelis as they hid inside. Hundreds were killed or taken hostage. It was the worst attack on Israeli soil since 1973. Many people wondered why the Mossad failed to anticipate such a large attack. Its scale was so vast that it must have taken months to plan. In January 2024, the leader of

OPPOSITE The Heron drone, made by Israel Aerospace Industries, can fly for almost 50 hours at a time.

the Mossad, David Barnea, vowed to hunt down and kill anyone involved in the October Hamas attacks. It may take years, but as shown by past missions, the Mossad eventually gets its targets. According to ABC News, as of April 2024, at least 1,700 Israelis had been killed in the fighting, including civilians, soldiers, and police.

The Mossad is one of the largest and most successful intelligence agencies in the world. It can strike with surgical precision and isn't afraid to exercise patience, often "playing the long game" with its missions. But the agency isn't perfect. It must continue to learn and adapt to an ever-changing world. One thing is certain: Surrounded by hostile countries intent on doing harm, the Mossad will remain vigilant and do whatever it takes to keep Israel safe.

Selected Bibliography

Ben-Hanan, Eli. *Our Man in Damascus: Elie Cohen*. New York: Crown Publishers, 1969.

Eisenberg, Dennis, Uri Dan, and Eli Landau. *The Mossad Inside Stories: Israel's Secret Intelligence Service*. New York: Paddington Press, 1978.

Follath, Erich, and Holger Stark. "How Israel Destroyed Syria's Al Kibar Nuclear Reactor." Salon. November 3, 2009. http://www.salon.com/news/feature/2009/11/03/syria_israel.

Hastedt, Glenn. *Espionage: A Reference Handbook*. Santa Barbara, Calif.: ABC-CLIO, 2003.

McGreal, Chris. "Israel Imposing Apartheid on Palestinians, Says Former Mossad Chief." *The Guardian*. September 6, 2023. https://www.theguardian.com/world/2023/sep/06/israel-imposing-apartheid-on-palestinians-says-former-mossad-chief.

Ostrovsky, Victor, and Claire Hoy. *By Way of Deception*. New York: St. Martin's Press, 1990.

Raviv, Dan, and Yossi Melman. *Every Spy a Prince: The Complete History of Israel's Intelligence Community*. Boston: Houghton Mifflin, 1990.

Rubin, Shira. "Israel's Top-Secret Mossad Looks to Recruit via Netflix, Hulu, and Apple TV." *The Washington Post*. December 18, 2020. https://www.washingtonpost.com/world/middle_east/israel-mossad-spies-netflix/2020/12/18/a48745d4-3f88-11eb-b58b-1623f6267960_story.html.

Glossary

agent — a person who works for, but is not necessarily officially employed by, an intelligence service

asset — a hidden source acting as a spy or providing secret information to a spy

bug — a hidden recording/listening device

covert — undercover or hidden

counterintelligence — efforts made by a nation's intelligence agency to catch and eliminate spies working against the country and protect the country against sabotage or terrorism; also called counterespionage

defect — to leave a country forever in favor of another

dictator — a person who rules with absolute power, often in an oppressive way

double agent — a spy for one country who doubles as a spy for a second country and often provides false information to the first country

drop a prearranged spot for dropping off and picking up information gathered through spying; also called a dead drop

espionage the act of spying

infiltrate to secretly enter in a gradual way, usually for the purpose of spying

intelligence intelligence uncovered and transmitted by a spy

mole an employee of one intelligence service who actually works for another service or who works undercover in a foreign country to supply intelligence

operative an undercover agent working for an intelligence agency

recruiting the process of hiring or enlisting

sabotage the act of purposely damaging or destroying something, especially for political or military gain

tradecraft the procedures, techniques, and devices used by spies to carry out their activities

traitor a person who betrays another's trust or is false to one's duty or country

Websites

The Institution for Intelligence and Special Duties

http://www.mossad.gov.il//Eng/AboutUs.aspx
Learn more about the Mossad directly from its website.

The International Spy Museum

https://www.spymuseum.org
Explore bios of real-life agents and frequently asked questions about spying.

Mossad

https://www.britannica.com/topic/Mossad
Read a brief history of the Mossad.

Index